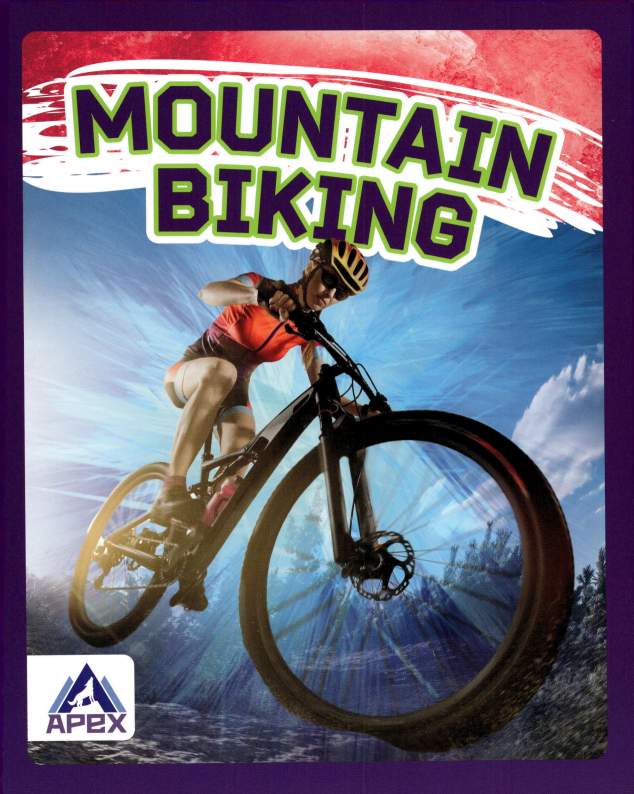

MOUNTAIN BIKING

BY MEG GAERTNER

WWW.APEXEDITIONS.COM

Copyright © 2022 by Apex Editions, Mendota Heights, MN 55120. All rights reserved. No part of this book may be reproduced or utilized in any form or by any means without written permission from the publisher.

Apex is distributed by North Star Editions:
sales@northstareditions.com | 888-417-0195

Produced for Apex by Red Line Editorial.

Photographs ©: Shutterstock Images, cover, 1, 4–5, 6–7, 8, 10–11, 12, 13, 14, 15, 16–17, 18, 19, 20, 21, 22–23, 24, 25, 26–27, 29; JP5/ZOB/Wenn/Newscom, 9

Library of Congress Control Number: 2021915730

ISBN
978-1-63738-152-6 (hardcover)
978-1-63738-188-5 (paperback)
978-1-63738-258-5 (ebook pdf)
978-1-63738-224-0 (hosted ebook)

Printed in the United States of America
Mankato, MN
012022

NOTE TO PARENTS AND EDUCATORS

Apex books are designed to build literacy skills in striving readers. Exciting, high-interest content attracts and holds readers' attention. The text is carefully leveled to allow students to achieve success quickly. Additional features, such as bolded glossary words for difficult terms, help build comprehension.

TABLE OF CONTENTS

CHAPTER 1
A THRILLING RIDE 5

CHAPTER 2
HISTORY OF THE SPORT 11

CHAPTER 3
MTB EVENTS 17

CHAPTER 4
PREPARING TO RIDE 23

Comprehension Questions • 28

Glossary • 30

To Learn More • 31

About the Author • 31

Index • 32

CHAPTER 1
A THRILLING RIDE

A rider balances at the top of a mountain. The starting horn blares. She zooms down the course. She's racing in a downhill mountain bike (MTB) event.

In many downhill races, riders use chairlifts to get to the starting line.

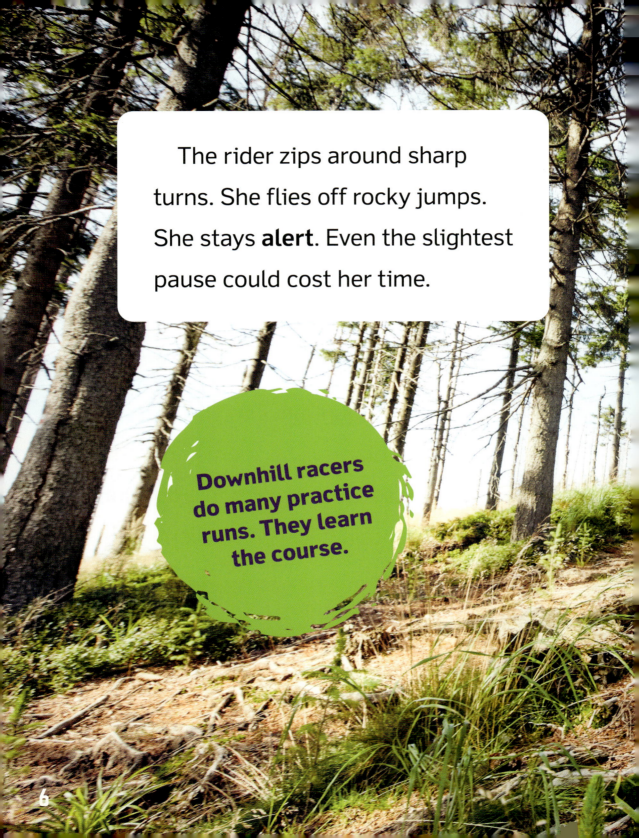

The rider zips around sharp turns. She flies off rocky jumps. She stays **alert**. Even the slightest pause could cost her time.

Downhill racers do many practice runs. They learn the course.

Riders go through a downhill course one at a time.

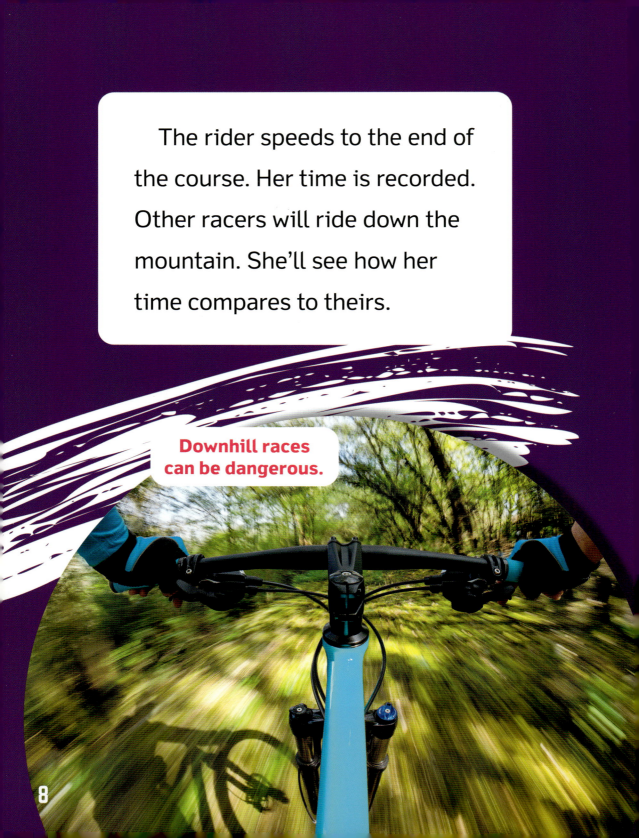

The rider speeds to the end of the course. Her time is recorded. Other racers will ride down the mountain. She'll see how her time compares to theirs.

Downhill races can be dangerous.

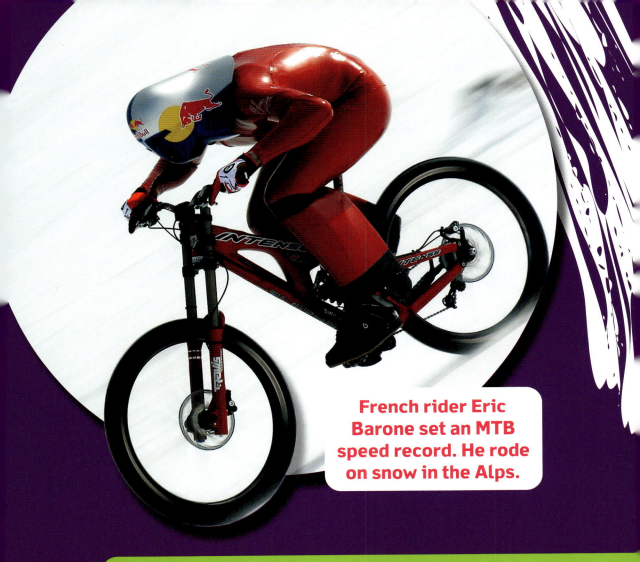

French rider Eric Barone set an MTB speed record. He rode on snow in the Alps.

NEED FOR SPEED

Downhill racers can reach speeds of 50 miles per hour (80 km/h). In 2017, a rider set a new record. He went 141 miles per hour (227 km/h).

CHAPTER 2
HISTORY OF THE SPORT

Teens invented MTB in the late 1960s and 1970s. They were seeking an **adrenaline rush**. So, they rode down a steep mountain.

Mount Tamalpais is near San Francisco, California. It's considered the birthplace of modern mountain biking.

The teens rode **modified** road bikes. They used thick balloon tires. They tested what worked best on rough **terrains**. Soon, their love of the sport spread.

Balloon tires were popular until 1959. Then skinny tires became common.

Early mountain bikers found lots of different bike parts. They used those parts to turn road bikes into mountain bikes.

The first MTB races happened in 1976.

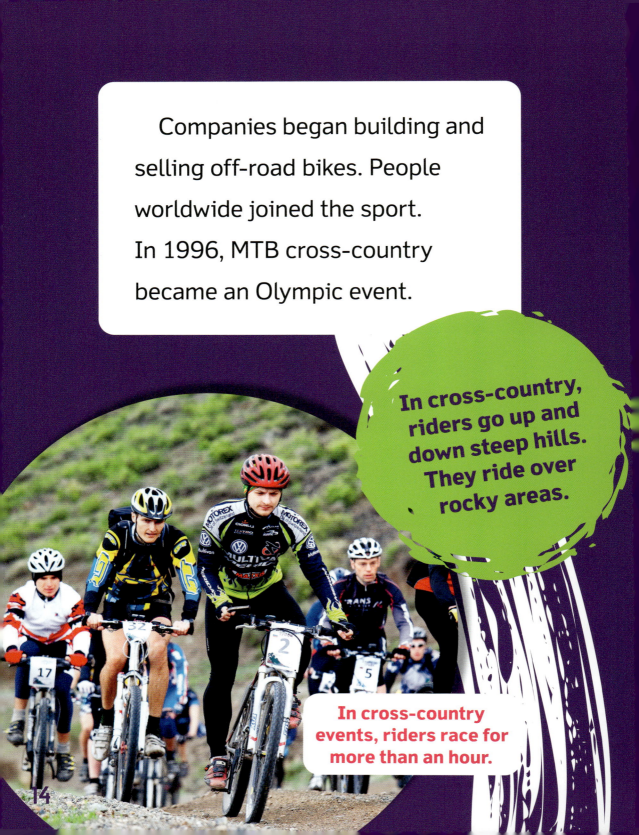

Companies began building and selling off-road bikes. People worldwide joined the sport. In 1996, MTB cross-country became an Olympic event.

In cross-country, riders go up and down steep hills. They ride over rocky areas.

In cross-country events, riders race for more than an hour.

MTB cross-country riders take part in the 2016 Olympics.

OLYMPIC RULES

Riders start at the same time. They do several laps around the course. After one lap, riders who are too slow are **eliminated**.

CHAPTER 3
MTB EVENTS

Cross-country and downhill aren't the only MTB events. In four-cross, four riders race head-to-head. The winner crosses the finish line first.

Four-cross tracks are similar to BMX tracks. Riders do several rounds of racing.

Other events are more about tricks than speed. Slopestyle riders fly off ramps. Then they do tricks. They spin their handlebars. They flip or spin.

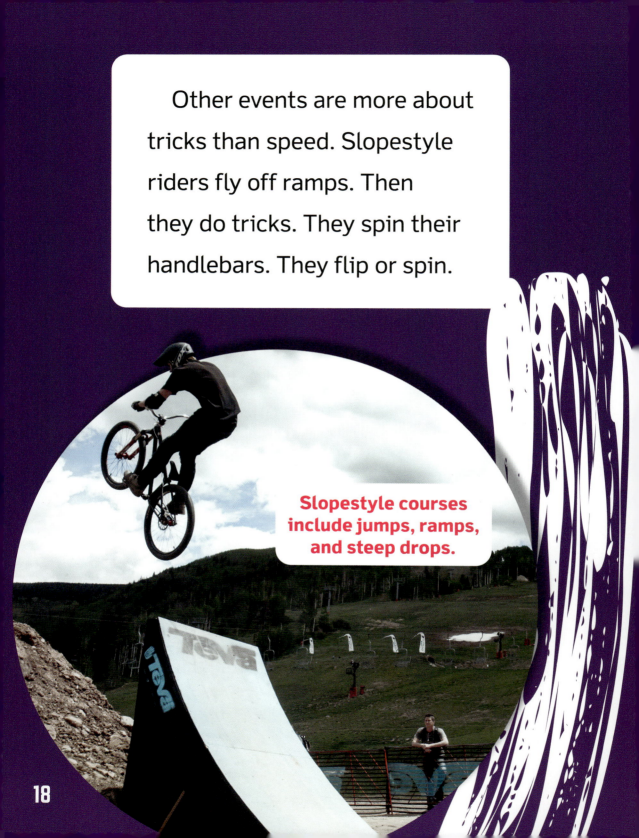

Slopestyle courses include jumps, ramps, and steep drops.

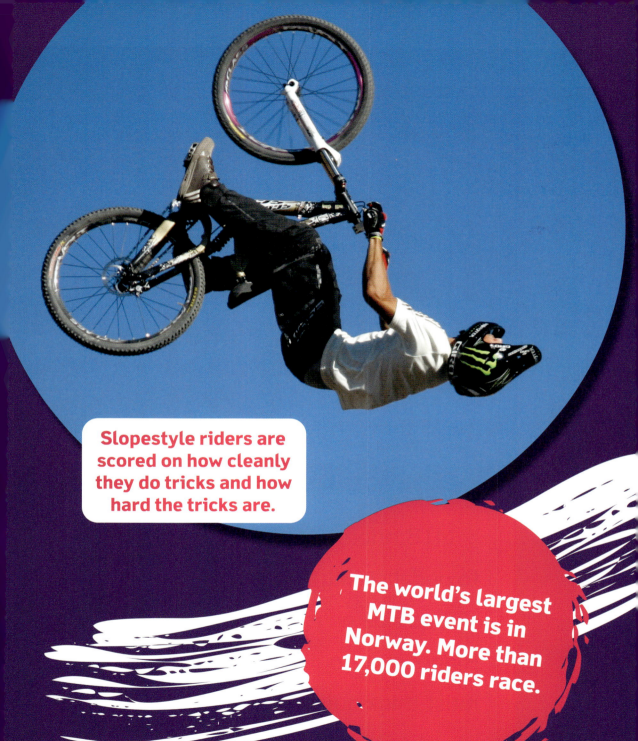

Slopestyle riders are scored on how cleanly they do tricks and how hard the tricks are.

The world's largest MTB event is in Norway. More than 17,000 riders race.

Mountain bikers often have to steer around trees, rocks, and other parts of nature.

MTB riders need strength to pedal uphill. They need skill to ride on rough terrain. Riders move quickly. They must think quickly, too.

ENDURO

Some MTB events require **stamina**. In enduro, riders race in several stages. They ride up and down mountains. But they're timed only on the downhill parts.

In enduro, the winner has the fastest time on all the downhill stages combined.

CHAPTER 4
PREPARING TO RIDE

Mountain bikes have thicker tires than road bikes. The tires also have rough **tread**. Some bikes have **suspensions**. These parts help make the ride smoother.

Tough, thick tires can handle rough off-road terrains.

Different bikes are built for different terrains. Cross-country bikes are light and fast. All-mountain bikes are good for steep rides downhill. They're good for climbing, too.

Hardtail bikes have front suspension only. All-mountain bikes are this type.

People can ride fat-tire bikes all year round.

FAT-TIRE BIKES

On fat-tire bikes, tires can be 4 to 5 inches (10–13 cm) wide. They are good for riding on snow or sand. People ride these bikes in some winter races.

Downhill riders should wear full-face helmets for extra protection.

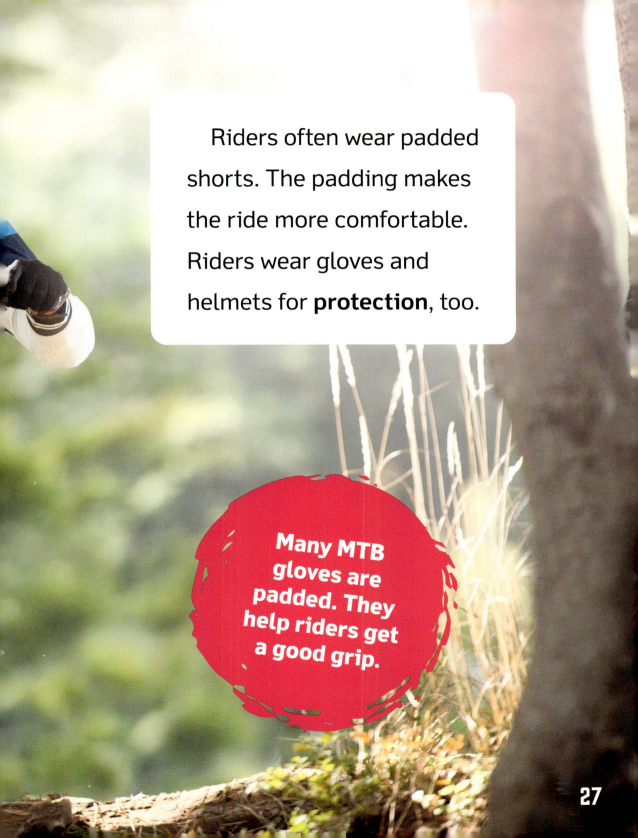

Riders often wear padded shorts. The padding makes the ride more comfortable. Riders wear gloves and helmets for **protection**, too.

Many MTB gloves are padded. They help riders get a good grip.

COMPREHENSION QUESTIONS

Write your answers on a separate piece of paper.

1. Write a few sentences explaining how the sport of mountain biking began.

2. Which MTB event would you most want to see? Why?

3. In which event do riders do tricks as they move through a course?

- **A.** slopestyle
- **B.** cross-country
- **C.** enduro

4. Why would good suspension be more important for a mountain bike than for a road bike?

- **A.** People ride road bikes over rougher terrains.
- **B.** People ride mountain bikes over rougher terrains.
- **C.** Mountain bikes have thinner tires.

5. What does **head-to-head** mean in this book?

*In four-cross, four riders race **head-to-head**. The winner crosses the finish line first.*

    A. with their heads touching
    B. at the same time
    C. at different times

6. What does **runs** mean in this book?

*Downhill racers do many practice **runs**. They learn the course.*

    A. sets of dance steps
    B. ways of writing
    C. laps on a course

Answer key on page 32.

GLOSSARY

adrenaline rush
A rush of energy from doing something daring and slightly dangerous.

alert
Quick to notice things or act.

eliminated
Removed from the race.

modified
Changed to be more suited to something.

protection
Something that helps keep people safe.

stamina
The strength to keep doing something that is hard or long.

suspensions
Systems on cars or bikes that protect people from feeling hard road or ground conditions.

terrains
Areas of land with different features.

tread
The part of a tire that touches the road or ground.

TO LEARN MORE

BOOKS

Abdo, Kenny. *Mountain Bikes*. Minneapolis: Abdo Publishing, 2018.

Jewitt, Kath, and Moira Butterfield. *The Ultimate Bike Book: Get the Lowdown on Road, Track, BMX, and Mountain Biking*. London: Carlton Kids Publishing, 2019.

Smith, Elliott. *Enduro and Other Extreme Mountain Biking*. North Mankato, MN: Capstone Press, 2020.

ONLINE RESOURCES

Visit **www.apexeditions.com** to find links and resources related to this title.

ABOUT THE AUTHOR

Meg Gaertner is a children's book editor and writer. She lives in Minneapolis, where she enjoys swing dancing and spending time outside.

INDEX

A
all-mountain bikes, 24

C
cross-country bikes, 24

D
downhill MTB, 5–6, 9, 17

E
enduro, 21

F
fat-tire bikes, 25
four-cross, 17

H
helmets, 27

J
jumps, 6

M
mountains, 5, 8, 11, 21
MTB cross-country, 14, 17

O
Olympics, 14

P
padding, 27

R
road bikes, 12, 23

S
slopestyle, 18
suspensions, 23

T
terrain, 12, 20, 24
tires, 12, 23, 25
tread, 23
tricks, 18

Answer Key:
1. Answers will vary; **2.** Answers will vary; **3.** A; **4.** B; **5.** B; **6.** C